ORAL

ELIXIR

Oral Elixir

By

Ausar

Lord of the Perfect Black

Oral Elixir by Ausar
Published by Aminia Books and Publishing
P.O. Box 783
Bridgeton, Mo. 63044
www.aminiabooksandpublishing.com

Cover designs by Aminia Books and Publishing
Cover graphics- Love Potion #9 by James Steidl

IBSN-10: 0-9799154-9-X
ISBN-13: 978-0-9799154-9-9
Library of Congress Control Number: On File

Printed in the United States of America

FIRST PRINTING

ACKNOWLEDGEMENTS

I want to give a "shout-out" to Kim Linzy, Yvette Smith, Troy(ATL), David "D-Poet" Jackson(STL), Abyss(ATL), Cocktails(ATL), Ron "Chill" Johnson(STL), Legacy(STL), the Young Messengerrzz(STL), Baba Kenya of the Harambee Institute of St. Louis, Tommie Bottoms (ATL), Talaam Acey, Freedom Speaks (ATL), Trisha "Quiet Storm" Martin(STL), Hope Stevens, Jon Goode(ATL), Love EZ(ATL), Ms-A-Divatude(ATL), Tiffany Smith, Mocha Latte "Got Lyrics?"(STL), 16 Bars (STL), Thunder & Lightning (STL), Craig B(STL), and all my family & friends in STL and the ATL!

SPECIAL THANKS

I must first give "ALL" thanks & praise to The Creator for blessing me with this tremendous blessing of poetry! I thank Him/Her for blessing me with the ability to take words, fuse them with emotions & experiences. This is truly a blessing! I WILL NEVER BETRAY MY GIFT! I have to give a very, very special thanks to my biggest supporter & encourager. She is my best critic and one of my best friends in this world. She has also been "the" inspiration for some of the pieces in this book. She was my co-host of "Open Oration", a spoken word show I produced & hosted in Atlanta. Therefore, to you, Kim Linzy, I say thank you very much! I Love You Very Much! Thank you for being there, and for being my friend!

A special thanks to Kirk, one of the owners of C'est Bon Cajun Restaurant in Atlanta. Kirk was responsible for getting the green light for "Open Oration" to take place at C'est Bon. Thanks brother! A special thanks to C'est Bon and the C'est Bon workers. I want to thank the awesome band of "Open Oration", Cliff O'Neal & Friends (Cliff O'Neal, Darryl Rivers, Ray West, and "Bass Man" Beard).

Thanks for your support. Thanks to Charles Beard, the official photographer of "Open Oration". Thanks to my man K.G. for hooking me up with Kirk. I appreciate you brother! Thanks go out to Princellar "Wild Angel" Bland, my sister and best friend. She is one of the best and most talented poets I know. Thank you for all you have done, I love you! Thanks to Pat Cheeks, Yvette Smith, The Afrikan Village, Dr. Ray "Doc" Hagins, Alyce Herndon, Cheri Pernell.

A very special thanks to Trisha "Quiet Storm" Martin for all you did in helping me in this process, and for your encouragement. Thanks to Ken Brown, Jayson & Wannie-Rose Williams, Dwayne & Tihara Williams, Ronnie Jackson, Gloria "54", Willie Ray, Wanda Wallace, Angie Johnson, Patrice Swank, Craig Johnson, Nadine Potts, Cynthia Curtis, Sherrell, Zylisha, and all the other sisters that inspired me.

Last but DEFINITELY NOT LEAST, Yulonda Brown "The Writer with a Purpose", thank you so very much sister for EVERYTHING YOU HAVE DONE TO HELP BRING THIS BOOK TO FRUITION! Thanks for sharing the pages in your wonderful book (My *Souls Desire*), with my poems! I am so honored that you felt my work was worthy of such an honor! For a writer to share the pages of their book with another writer is a HUGE honor. It also shines the light on your humbleness & humility as an artist. You have quickly become one of my best friends! I love you gurl!

The Eye of Heru

The Eye of Heru is the image that you see affixed onto each page of this book. The Eye of Heru symbolizes protection and the bringing of wisdom. The eye also symbolizes our ability to see with clarity and truthfulness. May you be able to see truth in all that is written.

TABLE OF CONTENTS

FOREWORD

Blessed to have crossed paths with many people, I feel I am well known, well liked, and very well respected. The only way that all of this has been attainable, is due to the character of man, in which I am. Many know the character & integrity that creates, Ausar. Not only here in the STL, but across the country. From the ATL to New York, Chicago, Memphis, Cleveland, and Dallas are just a few places; where my spirit and spoken word have been well received. Here is what one of my good friends had to say about Oral Elixir.

"Ausar is not only a writer, but a play write. He writes about love, lust, loss, and laughter on pages for all to feel! I often wonder who told him my secrets. These pieces are a sensual portrayal of love, sex, intimacy, and this bliss we call life.

Over the years, I've often had the privilege to experience his work. I've never read a piece that didn't move me. I don't know how he continues to write these full-blooded pieces, when it seems as though he just put all he had in the last piece! These pieces have spanned a lifetime. I believe they will continue to not only comfort, and excite, but also arouse us all for a lifetime.

I'm an avid reader, and I must say, that Ausar's body of work is a masterpiece of heartfelt poetry!"

Kim L.
Dallas, TX

Humbly speaking, there is only a hand full, if that many, that know the Soul of this man. The reason you ask. Raised by excellent parents, I was raised to be humble while yet, spiritually draped with confidence. Therefore, I was taught that is always best to "know" what I can do, and "show" it... to the best of my ability. My childhood teachings taught me, that it was not necessary to boast & brag about what I could do. I simply allowed my abilities speak for themselves. In doing so, the results encouraged others to speak on my behalf. I have applied my teachings, which is the approach I will continue to take in the world of Poetry and Spoken Word.

However, there are times when *"your"* voice has to be heard! The need for *"my voice"* to be heard, lead me to write *"Oral Elixir"* for many to medicate their souls for longevity in this crazy world. In addition, the realities of life continue to give me the confidence to perform on stage.

Oral Elixir is a way for me to speak for myself through my ability to orchestrate words & phrases into a soulful art form, known as poetry. Oral Elixir is the first of many doors that leads to the Soul of this man.

I will never speak about myself in general conversation, or in a one on one conversation. One of the keys to unlocking those doors is hidden in the words I write. Oral Elixir is not only a door to the Soul of this Silent Man, but it's also a key that can open other doors.

Oral Elixir is a necessary work. This door had to be opened. It had to be opened for the sake of the Silent Man. The Silent Man was imprisoned behind the door speaking to himself only. Allowing just a few people access behind the door to hear what his Soul had to say. Those few people attempted to bring him from behind the door, but with little success. Those few voices continued to echo in the ear of the Silent Man. Those few voices brought the Silent Man from behind the door, speaking that which he previously spoke only to himself. Those few voices gave him the confidence to speak aloud that, which was unspoken.

Oral Elixir is a culmination of accumulated years of unshared experiences, desires, disappointments, observations, lessons, and points of view. Oral Elixir, although entertaining at times, is a thought provoking work that must be thoroughly examined. It not only pulls the reader in, but also reveals a mirror for the reader to examine himself/herself.

Now, have a taste of *Oral Elixir*.

Ausar

Oral Elixir

Mom and Pop

In this section, these poems I dedicate to my mother and father. The first one is in honor of my mother, the greatest woman God ever put on this planet to me. She has been the best example of what a woman should be as a mother and a wife. She is the model for my next wife. I love her with every atom of every cell in my body! I love her with every once of energy that resides in my Spirit!

The second poem was a gift to me, from my father himself! He spoke to me in my Spirit a year after he made his transition. My pop was the strongest, greatest, most dedicated family man I ever knew. He had wisdom in him that I did not come to appreciate until after he left. Unfortunately, his prophetic warning about my lack of appreciation until he was gone came true. I miss him tremendously!

My Mother, God's Grace and Mercy

From the very inception in God's Mind
Of His Creation of me,
He already created the vessel
Thru which I would come to be.

In His wisdom placed He
All that was necessary in you
To nurture what already was
To bring about something new.

He taught you lessons
Previous to my life
To be used as ounces of prevention
To my future pain and strife.

He made you a mother
Long before you gave birth,
Then placed in you something that was nothing
And gave it worth.

You disciplined with love,
You protected without fear
You taught with a firm tongue,
And listened with a kind ear.

You became the standard by which
I will choose my wife.
You're the very essence
Of what a true mother should be.
You've been God's Grace, God's Mercy
To me in my life.

I'm Still Here

Although I'm not seen
With your eyes any longer.
The Spirit of love for God
And for self that I put in you
Shall make you stronger...

I'm Still Here

The lungs by which you breathe,
Are the result of my seed.
So every time you inhale and exhale,
Day after day, year after year.
Just remember...

I'm Still Here

The blood that flows thru your veins.
The heart that pumps it
From your feet to your brain.
In that same heart
That feels joy and pain,
I'll always remain...

I'm Still Here

So take comfort in knowing
That if you need to talk,
Guidance for the path that you walk.
Courage when you feel fear,
For that joy when you shed a tear.
Walk with confidence,
Don't cry, don't fear,
You're never alone...
I'm Still here.

Blackness

The Blackness Section deals with honoring our Ancestors, our people, and ourselves. It deals with our lack of conciseness, our shortcomings in terms of morality and spirituality. We must become stronger, more conscious, and more dedicated to the uplifting of our people to ensure the safety and perseverance of our children!!!

The Cry I Hear

Something's stirring about
Deep within my Spirit.
Voices in the distance
Listen close...can you hear it?

Our ancestors are crying
Because our children are dying.
So called leaders sold out
Because they're too busy trying
To be what they can never be,
Always denying...
So our children continue dying,
And our ancestors remain crying.

Go back and answer their cries,
Get the Truth
And return with a vengeance
To destroy the lies!

I hear the call of the drum
As warriors band together to fight,
To bring all Truth to light.
To defend that Truth with all their might.
And to kill or die...
For that very right.

I hear disappointment and anger
Because we refuse
To take heed to the danger.

The danger of
Not knowing the Truth,
Not living the Truth,
And not giving the Truth.
Listen brothers and sisters,
Listen to the call.
Sonkofa brothers and sisters...
Sankofa not just for yourself...
But Sankofa...for us all!

A Prayer for My People

This prayer is offered
In the many names
Of the One True and Living God.
The One Who commands The Universe.
The One Who demands
That we put Him/Her first!

My people are varied
In their religious and spiritual outlook.
Some are buried
By a falsehood taught to them by crooks.
They've been hoodwinked, bamboozled.
And took!

This prayer is for my people
Who sincerely try to do better
But aren't strong enough!
It's for those who get frustrated
With The Creator
Because they're patience isn't long enough.

This prayer is for the crack head,
And the wine head!
It's for the unconscious
Who's eyes are blind
And who's minds are totally dead!

This prayer is for the sister
That's selling her virtue.
It's for the teenage sister

Who violates her curfew
Because she hasn't mastered her nature,
So she's unable to resist temptation
And falls victim to
Pre-mature impregnation.

This prayer is for the brothers
Who think commonplace of
Every sister as a bitch,
A trick, and a hoe.

This prayer is to help
Get their mind back in line
So that they won't insult or disrespect
Your sister and mine.

This prayer is for my people
Who wish not to be who they are.
It's for my people
Who hate being what they are.
It's for my people
Who don't see their color
As a badge of honor,
But as some shameful scar.

This prayer is for my people
Who have lost their way.
It's for my people
Living day to day.
It's for my people
Who no longer believe in themselves.
It's for my people who have forgotten
Or no longer feel a need to pray.

This prayer is for those
Who before us came.

It's for those who suffered more...
But pushed forward just the same.

This prayer is for my people
Who died in the middle passage.
It's for my people
Who endured at the hands of savages.
It's for those
Who were wise enough to be quiet.
It's for those
Who were bold enough to speak out!
It's for those who refused
To remain enslaved,
Having a constant thirst for freedom
And stopping at nothing to seek it out!

This prayer is for Black Leadership.
Those of the past...
Those of the present...
And those that are to come.

This prayer is for "my" people!
Good, bad, or indifferent!
Who when the shackles are removed
And given the chance to excel...
Are never out done!!!

This Prayer Was For My People...
As'e.

A Monoxide Spirit

You never see me coming
Because I have no specific shape.
I smile, I hug, and I kiss.
You'd never believe
I'd commit spiritual rape.

Male, female
Can you tell the difference?
Or is there one?
Doesn't really matter,
The same damage is being done.

My spirit is toxic to the nostrils,
Yet there is no sense of smell.
Inhale enough of me
And you'll be looking up wondering
Just how you fell.

I don't have to be loud to be heard,
In fact I never am.
But your mind amplify my words,
And before you know it...
Your Spirit has become damned.

Now your ability to grow
Has become blocked.
The shackles of envy, jealousy and hate
Keeps your mind locked!

You're aware of my ability to kill,
But yet and still...
You let your guard down
When I come around
Allowing me to do as I will.

Now all of a sudden
It's you
Doing as I do...
No longer one
Now two.
Seeking out more
We now become four.
Continuing to multiplicate
The number now becomes eight.
And as long as we go unchecked,
Our numbers become even more great.
As we continue to devastate...
Annihilate...
And illuminate.
Thru envy, jealousy, and hate!

The Devil Laughs

While you sport and play,
Dance all night and day,
Soap opera your life away.
and not once did you stop to pray.

The Devil Laughs

While you Maury Povich & Jerry Springer,
Project your ignorance
Yet point the finger.
Stereotype your people
With no moral demeanor,
Refusing to do for self
Because you're a lotto dreamer.

The Devil Laughs

You shun the Truth and exalt the lie,
And when asked to explain...
You don't even know why.
Smoke your crack,
Induce can alcoholic high.
Convinced you're really living
Yet rapidly you die!

The Devil Laughs

While you snort your cocaine,
Foolishly seek world fame,
Publicly expose yourself
Without shame,
In your hand and in your forehead
You bare his name.

The Devil Laughs

You are warned
To seek forgiveness from The Creator
Because this world is going down fast.
but you say "no thank you, I'll pass",
And continue in your sinful crafts
All the while...
The Devil Laughs.

Love and Romance

There is really no explanation for this chapter. It simply is...what it is.

On Behalf of the Brothers

On Behalf of the Brothers
I'm here to "express"
in this open-hearted poem...
well it's more like to "confess".
Those things we keep to ourselves,
the secrets we keep tucked away on shelves.
and the reasons we yell,
The things we tell our boyz
when we're amongst ourselves.
First of all we...
Nah!
"Those" things I can never tell!
But here's what I can unveil.

1. The Things We Love About You:
We love the way you look,
the way you feel
and the way you smell.

The way you walk
the way you talk,
and the way you smile.

We love your confidence.
your imagination
and your style.

We admire your strength
and your ability to endure.

It's that "strength"
that we unwillingly lean on
when "we're" not so sure.

We love the way you hold us,
we love the way you console us.

We love the balance
you bring to our lives...
to make a "whole" us.

2. The Things We Fear:
We're afraid of losing your respect.
We fear not being able to
shelter and protect.

We fear your ability
to break our hearts
and crush our spirit.

We fear the courage it takes
to open our hearts
and let you near it.

3. What We Need From You:
We need you to stay strong,
we need you to stay confident,
we need you at our back!

We need you when we're down and out
and under attack!

We need that pat on the back
to make us feel good.
and we need that little "push"
that takes us from boy to manhood!

We need your smile when
ours is upside down.
We need you to keep us rooted...
to keep our feet on the ground.

4. What We Want:
We want to hold you,
make love to you.
We want to build a world
and place no one but God above you!

We want to spend time alone with you
in the home that we share with you.
We want to fulfill your every desire
just to let you know
how much we care about you.

We want to be all three things to you;
your friend,
your lover,
and your brother!
We want you Black woman!
You!... and no other!!!

Su Belleza Es Satisfactorio

Para ser capturado port u image
Me a dejado frezo
Ojos del tormenta.
Poderoso, implacalemente.
Para rechosar tu belleza...no es possible,
Para resistir es imposible!

"Su Belleza Es Satisfactorio"

Desde el tiempo
Nunca a sido...
La satisfaction de mi Corazon
Nunca a sido.
Nunca el sentimento a sido el mismo
Pero...
Es familiar como el aire que respido.

"Su Belleza Es Satisfactorio"

Nunca de Nuevo mis ojos buscoran
Porque el fin del paraiso termino...
Ojos caliente como el sol,
Sunrisa como la calmante breza.
Cabello como la coscada,
Todos sorbrendentemente junto
Un portfolio designado a satisfacer.

"Su Belleza Es Satisfactorio"

Desde el comienzo de tu cabeza
Asta el punto de su piez,
Su belleza en comparasion.
Para comsigir mi attencion?

Nada puede competir.

"Su Belleza Es Satisfactorio"

El sonido de su voce
Y el tono como me llama,
Monda un sentimento caliente
Desde el tombor de mis oido
Asta el fundo de mi Corazon.
Mandondome el necesario balor
Para resitir temptacion.

"Su Belleza Es Satisfactorio"

Her Beauty Satisfies (English Version of Su Belleza Es Satisfactorio)

To be captured by a look
Caught, frozen, still
Eye of the storm.
Powerful, relentless, unstoppable.
To deny her beauty...not probable,
To resist it...impossible!

"Her Beauty Satisfies"

From a time
Whence never cam
Has the fulfillment of my soul
Ever been greater met.
Never has a feeling been the same
And yet!...
It's as familiar as the air I breathe.

"Her Beauty Satisfies"

Never again shall my eyes wander,
For the search for paradise has ended...
Eyes as warm as the sun,
Smile as that of a gentle breeze.
Hair that flows like a waterfall,
All amazingly blended
Into one portrait designed to please.

"Her Beauty Satisfies"

From the top of her head
To the soles of her feet,
A beauty by comparison
To vie for my attention?
No other can compete.

"Her Beauty Satisfies"

The sound of her voice
And the tone by which she calls me,
Sends a warming sensation
From the drums of my ears
To the very chambers of my heart.
Giving me the necessary ammunition
To resist temptation.

"Her Beauty Satisfies"

Always...Amazing To Me

From the time whence
My eyes first beheld you
Til this very moment,
I remain under your spell Boo.

Around every corner
That you turn
As I'm engulfed by your countenance.
That familiar spark
Continues to burn.

Always...Amazing To Me

The feeling you gave me
When you made love to me,
Accompanies me in my sleep
And orchestrates my dreams.
It causes me to weep
In my imaginary pleasures
As I cream.

Always...Amazing To Me

I miss you
When I go off to work everyday.
That's why I call you
Every lunch break to say,
That if I had it my way...
Today would be my retirement day
And that way,
Every morning after breakfast
Back to bed we would return and stay.
You making love to me
In that special way,

Me screaming out your name
So fanatically.
The pleasure becomes too intense,
So I cry out for mercy
And at the same time
Commanding!
That you continue
Doing it that way!

My mind in total chaos!
and yet...so serene.

Always...Amazing To Me

The feeling of completeness.
That sense of uniqueness.
The very reason there's no need
To go outside our home to seek this.

It's all here with you.
Always...Amazing To Me.
Always...just us two.

Every Grain of Sand

Every grain of sand,
If weighted together
Against a single ounce of my love.
It would amass to no more than a feather.

Every grain of sand,
If stretched out in a single line,
Mile after mile.
Could never out measure
The lengths to which I would go
To give you satisfaction,
To give you pleasure.

Every grain of sand,
If put into a single hour glass.
Would first run out of time
Before I ran out on you...
Beautiful Black woman of mine.

Every grain of sand,
I would take and build you a castle.
A castle strong enough to carry
The weight of my love.
A castle filled with a million rooms,
And in each one I'd give you intense
pleasure
Well beyond measure.

A castle that would out live time.
That castle I'd build for you...
Because I love you...
Because you're mine.

Every Grain of Sand.

If Heaven

If Heaven
Ever had a smile,
It would be yours.

If Heaven
Were a kiss,
It would have to be yours.

If Heaven
Had a touch,
It would be exactly like yours.

If Heaven
Had eyes,
Their beauty would be that of yours.

If Heaven
Had lips,
They would be as shapely and as tender as yours.

If Heaven
Were an essence,
It would be like the one I find in you.

If Heaven
Was filled with passion
It would be of the kind that resides in you.

If Heaven
Was a desire?
It would be the kind that I feel for you.

If Heaven

Truly were a smile, a kiss
A touch.
If it had eyes, and lips.

If Heaven
Had an essence,
A passion and desire.
Then I can stay right here on earth,
There's no need to go any higher.

I don't have to wait until I die!
Heaven is here,
Heaven is now,
Heaven is you,
You're my Heaven.
You're Heaven everyday...
Standing right here...
Before my very eyes.

Every Time

Every time I see you
I smell you with my eyes,
I inhale you with intensity.
I yell out to you with inner cries
And fill with full blooded density.

Every time your vocal cords vibrate
Causing your tongue to curl
And your lips to shape the words
That would exude from your lungs,
My ears become erect!
And the hairs on the back of my neck!
Become stiff and direct!

Every time is every time
Time becomes ours
Yours and mine.
Every time began
The time you became mine

Every time I dream of making love to you,
Whether it be day or night,
The time is right.
Every time I imagine
Those lips...so tender,
That neck...no slender,
Those hips...so swervy,
That ass...so round and curvy.
My mind orgasms
Multiple times,
Each and every time!

Every time you walk...

~Oral Elixir~

As you're moving away,
My eyes are tattooed to your backside.
Studying the way it moves
As it bounces from side to side.

Every time is every time
Time becomes ours...
Yours and mine.
Every time began
The time you became mine.

Every time I'm away from you
Time stands at a distance.
But every time I'm with you
Time passes like an instant.

Every time I bed my sheets
To lay with you
I treasure every moment,
Every movement,
Every sway
As our bodies sensuously greet each other.

Every time I think of kissing you,
I begin missing you.

Every time is every time
Time becomes ours...
Yours and mine.

Every time is the time
I wish to spend with you.

Every time begins...with you.

You

Look at You,
behold You,
the shape of You...
a gorgeous woman, that's You.

Beautiful You,
sexy You,
delightful You...
the one who captures my eye, is You.

The feel of You,
the grip of You,
the squeeze of You,
is what I get in the arms of You.

When I kiss, there's You.
When I hug, there's You.
When I touch, there's You.
Making love to only You.

When I'm asleep, there's You.
When I awake, there's You.
When I think, there's You.
In my dreams, there's You.

The shoulder I cry on is You.
The ear I bend on is You.
The balance I weigh on is You.
On whose love I depend on is You.

The cause of my smile is You.
The cause of my laughter is You.
The cause of my joy is You.
The one that I love...is You.

~Oral Elixir~

The reason I live
is You.
All that I have
I wish to give to You.

In the morning
there is You.
In the afternoon
there is You.
In the evening
there is You.
Thru all the arguments,
trials & tribulations.
Thru all the disappointments,
still there is no leaving You.

I'll die for You,
kill for You.
And when I lay with You,
I'll thrill for You!

I'll tickle you
and tease You.
Lick You
and squeeze You.
Flip, toss, and turn You.
I'll do it all...
just to please You!

I'll grind with You,
69 with You.
Seek & find new ways
to blow your mind
with You!

I'll lay my heart on the line
for You.
Promise to be mindful to...
Love, Honor, and Treasure You.
Maintain, Protect, and Defend You.
From now...
until my life ends...
with You.

The Last One

To every end
there is a beginning,
But I could never have imagined
both being one and the same
and I'd end up winning.

Our beginning
was the end to all others.
No need to continue the search,
no reason to look any further.

You're the last one
I wish to kiss,
the last I'll ever miss.

You're the last one
I'll hold in my arms,
the last I'll ever charm.

You're the last one
I'll spend ever day with,
the last I'll ever lay with.

You're the last one
I'll touch in the middle of the night,
the last neck I'll gently bite.

You're the last one
I'll reveal my dreams to,
the last I'll put whip cream to.

You're the last one
I'll share a home with,
the last one I care to be alone with.

You're the last one
I'll give a ring to,
the last I'll ever cling to.

You're the last one
who'll make me laugh,
the last one to make me cry.
The last one to share my path,
the last one upon who's love I'll rely.

You're the last one,
the very last one.
My present, future,
And past one.

You're the last one...
The last one that'll "ever be".
The last one in my life.
The last one I want loving me.

You're the last one
I'll open my heart to.
That last and final part to
my complete happiness.
That Last One...is you.

Relationships

This chapter is my insight as to what we gather when dealing with one another on any level. Often times we tend to place relationships into one category. When in reality, the relationship may fall into many categories, in many different ways. We all have our own visions of what we want a relationship to be.

A fantasy of how we would like it to be. We can be committed to a relationship, attentive to a relationship and sometimes even unaware that a relationship exists! There is even the possibility that the relationship, never existed! Sometimes we betray or become betrayed in a relationship by pretending to be that which we are not. Whether the relationship is romantic, sexual, or spiritual, this section will cover it all.

20/20

What do you feel
When you see me?
How do I sound
When you hear me?

These are often asked questions
Of myself.
Answers that can come
Only from you...
you and no one else.

I ask them in silence
In a stealth type manner.
Hoping to see me
As you do.
Trying to get
An unselfish point of view.

With open eyes
I blindly look in the mirror,
But it's hidden from me.
Though I constantly asks...
What's so beautiful about me?
Like the fairy tale,
The answer is never

What I expect it to be.

I try to place
Myself behind your face.
Hoping to get a glimpse
Of something I've never seen before.
Hoping to hear those things
That I unintentionally ignore.

Trying not to be me,
So I can better understand me.
For the sole purpose
Of becoming a better me...
A more well-rounded me...
A more complete me...
To have a better appreciation
Of how you see me.

What's inside of me
You ask?
Often times I'm not even sure.
In my silence,
I ask myself.
If I were you,
And at the same time being me.
How would I respond
To the things I do?
Maybe, just maybe...
The answers would bring me
Closer to you.

Maybe the answers
Would help me better control my thoughts.
Thereby controlling my tongue
So fewer wars between us
Would be fought.

I think a lot of the questions
That I have about me,
Are deep inside of you.
The missing weight
That causes the imbalance
On the scale of self-harmony,
Can only be brought to bare
When I become aware
Of what's deep down in there.

I have to use both pair of eyes
To see the true me.
The eyes thru which you see me,
And the eyes of me.
Both of which I shall constantly
Improve my vision of me
By evenly using the two.
For the benefit of both
Me and you.

Self-image isn't true image.
It's ego-vision.
It's an unfinished portrait
Of the true picture.
And what you're looking at,
You can't really tell.
It not only distorts the model...
But the viewer as well.

20/20.

I Heard Your Silence

I heard you today
When you didn't say,
"I love you"
When you didn't say
"I need you"
When you didn't say
"I appreciate you".

You spoke to me loud and clear
When I didn't hear,
"I miss you"
When I didn't hear
"I really want to see you"
When I didn't hear
"I want to make love to you".

You made it plain to me
When I didn't see,
"that smile on your face"
When I didn't see,
"that sparkle in your eyes"
When I didn't see
"that happiness to be with me".

Silence speaks so loudly
By saying so little.
I can act so softly
While at the same time,
Being painfully brittle.

For those who are trained to hear
What “isn’t” said.
For those who are trained to see
What “isn’t” there.
Love can be a very hard thing to bare.

All Thru It All

From the very beginning
You could see,
That I was nowhere near perfect,
But it never stopped you
From loving me.

There were times when I was good,
Maybe even great.
It created a love in you
I thought would never dissipate.

But my arrogance steered me wrong
And I became blind,
Thinking "you" were the one
Who couldn't see.
Convinced that "you" committed the crime.

All Thru It All
You still loved me
All Thru It All

All Thru It All
You still consoled me
All Thru It All.

You gave me your love
On a silver platter,
Unconditional,
But it didn't matter.

You excepted my lies
Knowing they weren't true.
Hoping someday soon
That I'd do better.

Hoping someday soon
That I'd be faithful to you.

All Thru It All
You still loved me
All Thru It All

All Thru It All
You would still hold me
All Thru It All.

When you finally reached
The end of your rope.
When you finally decided to leave
Because you could no longer cope
With all that I was putting you thru.

I finally open my eyes
And suddenly realized,
That all I wanted was you,
That all I needed was you.

You walked away
Still in love with me,
But now...
More in love with you.

All Thru It All
You say you still love me
All Thru It All.

All thru It All
More than friends we'll never be
Because you can't forget
How I used to be.
Although you've forgiven me,
This is the way it has to be.
Separate and apart
But still having a special place
In your heart.

All Thru It All.

Forever Sorry

From the very moment
You left me
I know I would never
Again be,
In love with another
The same as I was
With you.

You left times before but,
You'd always return
Thru that very same door
To concede to reconciliation.
Casting away pride and ego
In favor of forgiveness
For rehabilitation.

At the time of your
Last leaving,
I anticipated your return
To offer more forgiveness
Of which I had grown accustomed
To receiving.

But on that very same door...
You decided not to knock anymore.

You never again
Stepped over that threshold...
Leaving our home silent,
Leaving our bed cold.

I came to you
Begging and pleading
"It's you alone

That I love!”
“It’s you alone
That I’m needing!”

But you said
The only thing you had left
To offer me
Was alone.
No more forgiveness,
No more home.

I begged you,
“Don’t let this time
Be the last.
I’m truly sorry
For all transgressions
Of the past”.

“All I need
Is one last chance.
I’ll never again
Victimize your love
With another unfortunate circumstance”.

But you said my chances don’t seem to last.
That my transgressions
Won’t stay in the past.
So I, along with them,
Must become a part
Of your past.

I eventually let go,
And decided to move on.
But I still wish
You were here.
I still regret your being gone.

Although I've grown
And can love once more.
There are times I wish
You'd come back...
Back thru that very same door.

Forever Sorry.

Ghost Lover

So many days I've spent wondering,
So many nights I've cried.
So many regrets I have
About how our love died.

You have no idea
Of how much I'm missing you,
The love we used to make,
The way it was kissing you.

I think about you so much
Til I ache for your touch.
Longing to wrap my arms around you
And squeeze you oh so much.

Dreams of you
Seem so real,
I can smell you in my sleep.
Convinced of what I feel,
I reach my peak
As pleasures intensify and increase.
Substitute satisfaction comes...
As I explode and release.

How often do I remember and discover
Sweet memories and new ways to recover,
The unattainable heart...
Of my Ghost Lover.

Doesn't matter how long it's been,
It's always wonderful to see you again.
I just wish I could give to you now
The kind of love I should've back then.

The kind of love and appreciation
That now exist,
In the past I chose to resist.

~Oral Elixir~

Never considered the fact that
One day you may be gone,
Take your leave of me...make your exit.

So you chose to do so
And I take full blame,
You had to go.
You did what was best for you.
I understand that now...
You couldn't take any more.

How often do I remember and discover,
Sweet memories and new ways to recover.
The unattainable heart...
Of my Ghost Lover.

A new life
You've vowed with another.
While I sit here and struggle
With misdeeds and indiscretions.
Wondering why it took so long
For me to learn my lessons.

Wondering why I had to pay
Such a heavy price and lose you.
Wondering..."what the hell was I thinking?
Why didn't I choose you?"

How often do I remember and discover,
Sweet memories and new ways to recover.
The unattainable heart...
Of my Ghost Lover.

My Ghost Lover.

Beyond

The vision of happiness
That presides in your mind
Has yet to come.
And you feel as though
It's so hard to find.

So now, beneath your nose
You've forgotten to look.
To busy reading the cover,
Instead of the contents in the book.

While you're trying to find the forest,
You're wondering...
"why are there so many trees?"
If I were to put it before you...
Would you see?

It's such a travesty
When you look beyond what's there,
Searching for your happiness everywhere,
And it can't be found anywhere.
But if you took the time
To make yourself aware.
You'd realize the only place you had to go...
Was nowhere.

I've always been...
Right there

Unaware

I had no idea
That it would be you.
Had no idea
That such desires
Were still true.

Convinced that...
Death made a claim
On that part of my heart.
And my tongue echoed the same.

Trying desperately
To maintain control
Over something that has
Quickly penetrated my soul.

It's a beautiful feeling
To have deep attraction,
A growing friendship
With similar interest
And yet...that's just a fraction.

So much more to learn.
So much more to look forward to.
So much more to be had.
So much more...to me and you.

A Delicate Separation

Always friends,
But never lovers.
Although at times
I do discover,
You're in my mind
In places that are sacred.
Those places filled
With erotic fantasies.
Those places that require us
To be naked.

But I digress...
Let me re-structure
My thought process.

Because when I allow myself
To visit those places
That are sacred.
I put us both at risk.
And our friendship is far too valuable
To forsake it.

It's much easier to lose a lover,
Than it is a friend.
And if we ever cross that line
And it doesn't work...
Our friendship would never again
Be the same.

Lovers come...
And lovers go.
But friendships sustain,
And continue to grow.

But I must admit though,
Unprovoked thoughts of you
Have caused me to lose
Track of time.
Moments lost
With the thought of you.
Patches of time gone
Because of you.

But I guess it's better
To relish in my fantasies,
Because with them
I have total control.
With them...
At any given moment
Your tender hand I can hold.
With them...
I can summand your smile.
A smile that warms my soul
Whenever I'm feeling lonely and cold.

Our friendship is safe,
And it never disappoints.
It's not argumentative.
And it gives us more
Of what we need,
As opposed to what we want.

It's a pillar of strength
That we can lean on.
It's a kind ear
That we can bend on.
It's a confidence...
That we can depend on.

But I've always

~Oral Elixir~

Looked at you
In a personal light,
A physical light.
I don't know
If that's wrong or right but,
From the very first moment
I laid eyes on you,
It felt natural...
It felt right.
Although that line
Has never been crossed.
Maybe one day...
We just might.

So until that day comes.
If that day comes.
The delicate separation
Shall remain.
And our "friendship"
Will continue to be the mainframe
Of what binds us...
Keeps us...
Holds us together.

Til when and if
There'll be a crossing over
Of the separation
That exists between us
That's so delicate.

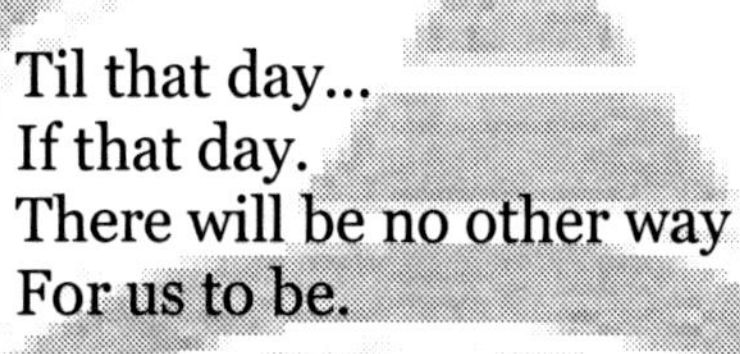

Til that day...
If that day.
There will be no other way
For us to be.

Forever friends.
Forever the delicate separation...
Forever...
We'll always be.

You Like It When I Pretend to Love You

I've given you evidence,
And I know you've seen it,
That my heart isn't in this thing.
I've clearly told you things
And didn't mean it.

I've shown you through my actions
That I don't always mean what I say.
I've apologized for doing you wrong,
Promised not to do it again,
And turned right around and did it anyway!

I've stood you up,
Or showed up extremely late.
I call you when and if I feel like it,
And have repeatedly postponed
Or cancelled dates.

And still you love me!
Why?

I've heard your tears on the phone,
Hell, I've sat there and watched you cry!

Often times I'm hard and cold
In spite of the warmth and affection
You so generously offer.

I ask myself
Why do you stick and stay?
What's keeping you here?
Why haven't you gone away?

Why do you put up with some of the things
I do?

I'll tell you why...
because You Like It When I Pretend To
Love You.

At any given moment
I may grab you and squeeze you tight.
I might wake you with oral satisfaction
In the middle of the night.
I might surprise you with a new outfit
And a brand new pair of shoes.
Or take you along with me
And let you choose.

You like those tender moments
When I express how much I need you,
And how much I love you.
Those words are precious to you...
They feed you.

Although those moments are rare
And don't come very often.
You remind yourself of them
When you're heart is hard
And needs to be softened.

Because you dread the thought
Of losing me
And giving someone else the chance
Of choosing me.

You Like It When I Pretend To Love You.

You give life to my words

Like God gave wings to birds.
You take them and fly!...Soar!
And go far beyond their true meaning
And what they were intended for.
Anytime I sense your feelings
Are approaching death.
I resuscitate them
Back to life with my breath.
Inhaling hope
So you can once again
Exhale your dreams.

Dreams of you and I together
Happy one to the other
Forever.
No chance of us being apart...
Never!

You Like It When I Pretend To Love You.

Don't misunderstand me,
I do care.
But not to the degree
That you would like it to be.
But I do care enough
To want you with me.

Deep down in my heart
You know this to be true.
But you choose to ignore it because
You Like It When I Pretend To Love You.

Lyrotica

What is Lyrotica? It is oral foreplay given in the form of words. Words placed together to entice, enhance, arouse, and tease. It is oral sex without touching! Lyrotica, is the use your mouth to make the other person literally "feel" that which you are going to do to them...by licking them up and down with your words!

~Oral Elixir~

Speak to Me

You may wonder why
I call you so much,
Or why I prefer a soft whisper
Along with your touch.

You often ask...
Why do I look at you in that way?
Even when it's meaningless
Trivial things you say.

It really doesn't matter
What you say,
Just Speak to Me.
Your voice soothes me so,
It moves me...oh!
Speak to Me.

Your voice has a rhythm
That vibrates my soul,
Mellows the beat of my heart...
A sound that'll never grow old.

A melody...
That gets better with time.
A sound...
As sweet as wind chimes!

It really doesn't matter
What you say,
Just Speak to Me.
Your voice soothes me so,
It moves me...oh.
Speak to Me.

~Oral Elixir~

When you're away…
I often replay the things you say
Just to carry me
Thru the day.

Speak to Me.

From the very moment
You said hello,
I knew
I never wanted to let you go.

That was it!
I would never belong to any else,
I was yours…
Once and forever more.

Speak to Me.

When you awake in the morning
Speak to Me.
When you lay down at night
Speak to Me.
When we make love
Speak to Me.
When you squeeze me tight
Speak to Me.

If ever you want to please me,
Even if it's just to tease me…
Speak to Me.
Just Speak to Me.

Just… Speak to Me.

Whispers In Silhouette

Candles emerge from the darkness
Changing both light and shadow.
A sensuous meeting of the two,
In like manner of when
My eyes greeted you.

I choose my words carefully
As not to offend.
I select a tone that's
Pleasing to the ear...
Just warm enough to make it bend.

As I come closer,
Reflections move and dance.
The attraction gets stronger
As your beauty is enhanced.

Your fragrance is teasing me,
Your smile is pleasing to me.
Your response is telling me
That my eyes weren't deceiving me.

Self-introduction is made
Softly in your ear and as I'm saying,
How captivating you are
In that outfit you're displaying.
You listen intently
As my tongue is swaying,
Analyzing every word
For signs of me betraying,
But silly games and schemes
I'm not interested in playing.

My goal is to go beyond
Your pretty face,
Discover your mind
To see if it's in a proper place.
To measure your self-worth
By letting you set the pace.
Now I'm analyzing your words,
Your character...
For style and grace.

What's left to be found?
We know not yet,
But the search has begun...
Whispers in Silhouette.

Your Pillow

As I lay here
And watch you sleep.
I wonder what are your dreams?
What secrets do they keep?

What communication is being shared?
Who talks to you?
What are they saying?
Whispers beneath your head
Directly in your ear.
Maybe it's something your pillow said.

In your absence
I attempt to go where you've been
So I place my ear upon your pillow,
Hoping the same things
Would be said again.

My love for you
Is so strong and so deep,
That I'll follow you anywhere...
Even into your sleep.

I wanna dream your dreams.
I wanna think your thoughts.
I wanna know what joys you've had,
And what wars you've fought.

I wanna place my nose there
So I can inhale
What you've exhaled.
Intake the reactions you've expelled
So that I can love you
On another level,

In another realm.

I wanna count the times you've cried.
I wanna count each and every tear.
I wanna know
So I can go back and ease the pain.
I wanna be there
To protect you in times of fear.

I wanna leave that part of me in your pillow.
So every time you go there,
I'm there if you need me.
I'm there in whatever capacity

You need me to be.

When you dream of making love to me.
I wanna feel it in "my" sleep!
I wanna share that moment with you.
I wanna feel every stroke!
Long...Hard...and Deep!

I long to know your every wish
So I can fulfill the demand
Long before you give the command.
Give you every confidence
That not only am I willing to but,
Knowing even more so...
That I can.

So you see,
Your pillow is not just a place
You lay your head to sleep.
It's a place for secrets to keep,

A place where dreams are buried deep.

It's more than a tool for comfort.
More than something
That makes a bed complete.

Your Pillow.

Things You Don't Know About Me

As well as you may know me,
There are some things
Yet to be found.
Like the things I do
When you're not around.

Not to exclude those moments
When you're here.
Those unspoken thoughts and fantasies,
Every time you come near.

When I watch you walk,
I study every step,
Outline every curve.
I ingest every bounce
In my mind,
Imprint every swerve.

I time the rhythm
Of when your arms swing
In sequence with how
Your hips sway.

It's a beautiful thing
To watch you coming but,
Even more delightful
To see you move
As you're walking away.

To hear your name mentioned.
And it doesn't have to be
In reference to you.
I just light up inside.
I reminisce on the things you do.

And my happiness is displayed
Thru a smile I can't hide.

During those times when you're ill,
Or in any type of pain.
My worry and concern I can't contain.

Although you're accustomed
To seeing me calm, cool, and in control.
What you're unaware of
Is my desire to take it all away.
A desire that burns deep inside my soul.

When I'm home alone
And missing you,
As I often do.
I create your presence
Thru artificial means.
Your perfume I'll smell,
Your pillow I may hold and cling.

I'll nap on the side of the bed
In which you sleep.
I'll lay my head on your pillow
Trying to dream your dreams...
Damn that's deep!

I'll play your favorite song
Trying to hear what you heard.
I close my eyes and become you...
I'm listening intently to every word.

I stare at your picture
And recall the first time we met.
Remembering those times
I didn't think we were going to make it

And yet...
We're both still here.
No matter how tough times seemed to get!

I can't go a day
Without hearing your voice.
Not one day without your smile.
Never a day without your touch.
You're my One,
There is no other choice!
I could go on but...
There's just so much!

All the things I experience and do
As a result of you,
Can't be contained in one poem
No matter how much I consider myself a poet.
The things you don't know about me
I may never tell.
And the ways
That they are displayed...
I'll never show it.

Private Moments

As I drift thru
The prized moments of my imagination.
A two cast ensemble starring you and I.
Screenplay setting of hugs, kisses,
And...other such recreations.

Alone in my bed,
But never in my mind.
As I recall time after time,
While pleasures with oil to anoint.
My head drippin
With the wisdom of satisfaction.
If you think
I just had a religious experience
Then you're missing the point.

During the moments of your absence,
I crave your scent, your touch,
Your lips, your voice,
Your essence, your energy,
Of which there is so much.

You could be at work,
Or sitting in your car,
In the very next room,
You don't have to be far.

You could be anywhere
And be totally unaware...
That you're making love to me,
And you're not ever there.

Your past deeds to satisfy
Are what I call on when I...

~Oral Elixir~

Feel the need for your presence
And you can't attend.
So I proceed to love without you...
Over and over again.

You can pleasure me without effort
When you're not around.
I can still feel every stroke,
Recall every scream, every whisper,
Every pleasurable sound.

Driving in the car
On my way to see you.
I've already completed the trip,
Looked into your eyes,
Held you close...
And kissed your tender lips.

So when I arrive,
Everything we're gonna do
I've already rehearsed.
The reason I take such care to please you,
Is because you've already pleased me first.

Private Moments.

Erotica

All the nerve tingling, body bending, physical, mental, and verbal stimulation that goes on between the ears. Be it in between the pages of this book, or the sheets, there is one thing I can promise you. When passion, desire and the opportunity to release with one another is present, the episode becomes explosive.

Hunger

I'm starving,
I'm cravin.
My appetite is intense
Cause I've been savin.

Now I'm wishing and praying,
Between your luscious thighs
I could be laying.
Intense strokes of
Simultaneous rhythms
With hips swaying.
Satisfaction you're relaying
Thru your lips saying...
This type of déjà vu
Should be everyday and...
No one has ever
Made you feel this way and,
You crave more orgasms
With no delaying!

Make 'em multiply
Single, double, triple.
Your body's on a sexual high.

Hunger
A touch, a taste, a smell.
Why?

No matter yet,
How?

Oh I remember.
It started when we first met.

Then after that
The hunger grew and grew.

I thought less
About my inhibitions,
And more about
All the things
I was now willing to do.

The Hunger

At that very moment
I realized,
Though the hunger
Was in "me".
"Your" satisfaction
Was the real prize.

Until I met you
I never knew
How misguided was my cravin
So that's why I started savin.

Although my hunger is controlled,
I can't ignore the urge.
So with a healthy diet of you,
Constant and steady.
There'll be no unnecessary surge.

With a healthy diet of you
Morning, noon, and night.
My hunger stays in check
While giving satisfaction
To my appetite.

With a healthy diet of you,
All that's needed on the menu
From appetizer, entrée, to dessert.
Is you, you, and you.

Oh yeah...
And come again Thank you!

I Have a Taste for Some...

When I awake with you in the morning
And res-erection has taken place.
Three things come to mind...
My tongue, your clit, my face.

The most important meal of the day
Can be prepared in 69 ways.
As your mouth is full
And my tongue sways.

I have a Taste For Some...

A sexual buffet
Full of tasty treats.
Strawberries, whip cream, and cherries.
Honey, chocolate syrup, along with other sweets.
All displayed on a table of you.
Hot...fresh...and ready to eat!

I Have a Taste For Some...

From the top of your head,
To the very toes on your feet.
I will kiss, lick, nibble, and bite.
Til my job is complete.

Please, just call me
Whenever you feel the need to be...
Just pick up the phone!
You can have it anywhere you want it!
Outside in the park,
Backseat of the car,
At the front door at home.

Ah, yes, I Have a Taste for Some...

I love to hear that sound.
The sound of your screamin,
As you're creamin.
Your love steady drippin
As I'm constantly lickin.
It's all over my lips and...!

I Have a Taste For Some...

P.U.S.S.Y.

What is Pussy? Pussy is...

Pleasurable
Uninhibited
Sensuous
Sensations
Yearning for more.

Pussy is...

Passions
Unleashed
Seductively
Said
Your way.

Pussy is...

Palatable
Undeniable
Sweetness
Screamin
Yellin for mercy.

Pussy is...

Pleasing
Unified
Spirits
Solidifying
You and I.

Pussy is...

Poetic
Uplifting
Spectacular
Rsounds
Yoked together.

Pussy is...

Powerful
Unmistakable
Supreme
Superlative
Yes, all that.

Pussy is...

Prescribed
Unavoidable
Succulent
Secretions
Yummy to my tongue.

Pussy is...

Perfect
Unlimited
Supple
Softness
Yielding to my hardness.

Pussy is...

Positively
Unequivocal
Silky
Smooth
Youthfulness

Pussy is...

Praiseworthy
Unrestrained
Spectacular
Squeezes
Yet not constrictive

Pussy is...

Portrait

Candlelight Silhouette
Smoked mirror reflections
Satin sheet movements
Causing an erection.

Rose petal bathwater
Wrapped in a terrycloth robe
Pear glaze body lotion
Tantalizing my nose.

Red trench coat
Black lace camisole
Thigh high silk stockings
Stiletto heels...six inches tall.

A standing point of view
Watching you work down south
Hand on the back of your head
As I slide in and out of your mouth.

Face to face
You calling my name
Confessions of love are made
As I'm doing the same.

Portrait.

Picture This

Visualize...
Fantasize...
Listen...because I want you to conceptualize
The many things I see
When you stand in the light of my eyes.

Teasing me,
Pleasing me.
Mental images of you & I intertwined...
Seizing me.

Imagination arrested...
Freezing me.
In a place
I long to be physically.
Desperately longing to make that place
a reality.

Picture this.

Lips moist and wet,
Breast full and erect.
Between your thighs you sweat
Images only in my mind and yet...
All three provide a real place
For me to lay my face...
To sample and to taste.

Just let me taste it.
I promise I won't waste it.

Let me kiss you there,
Down there where it counts.
I swear I'll drink every ounce.

~Oral Elixir~

Can you picture this?

I don't want you to just feel
My velvet tongue sliding
Across your clit.
Or the full blooded stiffness of my dick
Separating your slit.

I also want you to feel,
I mean truly feel,
The level of energy I'm producing
To keep your energy level high.
To make sure orgasms
Are constantly reproducing.

You're more than a picture.
You're a masterpiece
With no need for a frame.
Because your sensuality and your erotica
Has no borders.
And therefore can't be contained.

You're more than erotic,
More than sensual,
More than sexual.
You're an education
Mastered in all three
With a degree...
For satisfying me.

Description

Five senses,
Five ways to describe.
The most basic instincts
Five proofs of being alive.

If asked to describe love
In five ways.
How many would you find?
How descriptive could you be?
Would you leave any behind?

Do you believe
In love at first sight?
If you're easily
Captured by beauty,
A handsome face, a fine booty.
Then you just might.

The aroma
Of a seductive perfume,
A sexy cologne.
Of all the scents in the room,
"that one" stands alone.
Pulling you in
Like a bee to a flower.
Buzzed by it's power,
Minute after minute...
Hour after hour.

A voice so sweet,
A sound so dep.
A tone that causes you to melt,
Sensations in the ear
Like you've never felt.

~Oral Elixir~

The things said are amplified,
Untapped desires
You can no longer hide.
You heed to the command,
Unable to resist the demand.
Forever a slave
To that tone, that sound.
Forever bound.

Is it really possible
To put into words
The feeling of the right touch?
Why is it you can't explain
Why one person's
Power over you is so much?

Not even a dictionary
Can define
The feeling in your mind,
The sensations,
The heart palpitations,
The excitement,
The electricity
While having intimate relations.

Love can be palatable.
Sweet and moist,
Soft and wet,
Tender and yet...
As creamy as ice cream
When it first starts to melt.

Have your senses
Come alive?
Can you count to five?
Was there an extra one?
Count again...
Surprise!

Description.

Touch

The very tip of my fingers
Tingle and come alive
As they mingle and glide
In scented oils and black skin.
Massaging and caressing
Covering every curve,
Releasing all tension within.

"I'm talking about Touch"

As I look into your eyes
I start to fantasize...
Knees pointing high
Intense passionate cries
Ten toes in the sky!

"Can you imagine it? Touch"

As we're rocking and reeling
Climbing walls to the ceiling,
Bed bouncing and squealing
Deeper and deeper I'm drilling,
Your inner muscles contract
To intensify the feeling!

"Touch"

With every sight of you
"Touch"
With every thought of you
"Touch"
With every scent of you
"Touch"
On every part of you
"Touch.

Close Your Eyes...and Just Listen

Here we are
Just us face to face.
Nothing else exist...
Nothing else matters.
Just us here in this place.

The mood is set,
The music is soft and light.
Anticipation is high,
Your muscles are all tense...
Stomach all uptight.

Just relax
And let me take charge.
Allow me to calm you down.
It's not that hard.

Lay back and breathe easy.
Concentrate and unclench your thighs.
Uncurl your toes,
And close your eyes.

Feel the music
And listen to the words I say.
Surrender your body to me
Unconditionally, in every possible way.

What I'm asking may sound simple but,
It's much deeper than that.
My request demands
More than just your attention, in fact.
It goes straight to the heart
Of your trust.
And that's something I cherish.

So you don't have to feel pressured,
You don't have to feel rushed.

I'll start with a light massage.
Gently rubbing the temples of your head,
Down your neck, over your shoulders,
And all the way down to your feet.

Continuing on
Pass your calves, between your thighs,
Slowly over your breasts,
And back to your head.
Would you like some more?
Enough said.

This time around
I only wanna hear one word.
When I touch a nerve,
You know...hit that spot.
Immediately call out to me.
Stop!
And I'll focus all my energies there.
Intensify the sensation,
Before I proceed elsewhere.

Can you feel the music
Your "body" is make?
I can.
I feel every rhythm,
Every definitive beat!
A chorus of sensations singing to me,
"I'm yours for the taking"
No other song ever sounded so sweet.

Listen and concentrate
Because I'm about to penetrate.

~Oral Elixir~

Can you hear the rhythm
"my" body now makes.
You can count the beats
With every stroke I take.

Hear the way that I enjoy you.
Listen to the sensations as I explore
All up inside you.

Feel my chorus
Getting stronger and stronger!
Feel my note
Getting longer and longer!

How many measures can we go
Before the song ends?
How many measures...
Before we play it again?

Close your eyes...and listen.
Listen to the love we make,
Listen to the sound my tongue makes.
Count how many licks it takes
Before you explode
Quiver and shake.

Close your eyes...and listen.
As beads of sweat roll off your body
And glisten.

Close your eyes...and listen.
Listen to the sound of sleep
As it comes near.

Close your eyes...and listen.
Because when you awake
My voice will be the first sound you hear.

Close Your Eyes...and Just Listen.

Expending Energy

A darkened candle-lit bedroom
She slowly walks in
The sweet smell of perfume precedes her
Bring to full attention
That which is my outward extension
Being to her
A full invitation
To join me in a journey
No, no, a quest!
To please herself atop
And proclaim herself the best.

A change in position
As the quest continues
Names reverberate
Passionate cries are heard
As toes curl and legs shake.

Flesh exploding against flesh
Body oils and sweat...
Do you wish to climax?
No, not yet!
She request more time
So higher and higher she could climb
Her nails embedded at the base of my spine
And when I asks her how's it is?
She willing tells me...
It's mine, it's mine, it's mine.

Once again
Positions change,
Back flat
And knees high
My face thigh deep in the "Y"...

Tongue so warm
And feels like velvet,
Climax comes
Like that of a tidal wave
Toes clinch, hang ten,
Another is about to begin.
Clinch it...,hold it...,
Ride it out.

And that is just a small portion
Of what "Expending Energy"
is all about!

Even More Energy

As I arise once again
You turn over and invite me in,
The smell of perfume and sex
Combine and blend
Fully awakening the senses while...
As I'm pumping it in.

Intense strokes
Of flesh pounding
No room for silence
As screams of pleasure
And headboard sounding...
You talk back to me
My name repetitiously resounding
Off the same walls
That I have you climbing
Now all of a sudden you're finding
Multiple orgasms that are reminding
You of the love that you feel for me.

By the reaction of your body
It's nothing but real to me
And such a thrill to be
In your sacred place
Causing me to get that look on my face...
That only you can bring.

But I'm not ready to exit now
So I hold back...
Control is easy
When you know how.

Before I release
There's an area of concern
To that which I must return.

The quest would not be complete
Without your favorite treat
A journey to that place
Between X and Z...?
You know...Y
I wonder what look is on your face
While mine is deep in the thigh.

Ecstasy fulfilled
Because my woman is thrilled
That her energy wasn't wasted
But instead...
Well taken care of
And thoroughly tasted!

Degrees of Difficulty

No allowance
To love and admiration.
Nonchalant and carefree...
That's my situation!

All appearances
Seemingly content,
Outwardly cool.
Maybe to some extent but...
Myself I can never fool.

Not offering any opposition
But, not accepting
Of the proposition.

Doesn't matter
Who's propossin
My emotions
Are frozen

All the rules
Of freedom and independence applied
Strongly enforced,
And on their strength..
I heavily relied.

All of a sudden
Came you.
Degrees of difficulty
Came tumbling down.
What am I now to do?

I haven't visited this place
Of vulnerability in such a long time.

I'm fearful.
I want to cross back over
To my place of safety,
But I can't find the line.

Well I'm here now.
So I'm depending on you
To protect my heart
And keep me safe.
It's you I'm relying on
To keep me in a happy place.

All my hidden desires,
All my repressed needs
Re-introduce themselves to me.
Reminding me of myself...
The lover I truly wish to be.

So I organize
All these thoughts,
These needs and desires.
And place them happily
At your feet.
This is the real me...
Complete.

You reveal to me
Your degrees of difficulty,
And cautiously step around
That which I placed at your feet.

You say the things
That over came me,
Are not acceptable to you.
That's not a place
You wish to be.

Your attempts to be
Gentle and consoling,
Fall short of my
Pain and disappointment
Of which I am
No longer controlling.

Difficulty to another degree
Presents itself before me.
I must re-gain control
Over that which now has
A hold of me.

I must step away!
I have to be
Who I was yesterday!
Because my heart...
Will never survive...
Another replay.

Solitary Confinement

I'm confined,
Confined in a prison with doors
That lead to nowhere.
A prison with cold, unforgiving
Concrete floors.

Searching endlessly it seems,
For light completely in the dark.
My sleep visited by violent dreams
Tearing my mind apart.

I can't escape the madness
Because I can't stop the sadness!
I'm grasping the empty darkness
As I'm reaching for the imaginary spark
ness!
Both hands empty except for...
The tears I shed
As I attempt to pen knob less doors.

It seems as though,
My prayers are unheard.
My soul screams for an answer!
In the proceeding results
Of all my efforts...
"No" is the word.

A prisoner of my own freedom.
A slave to the emancipation
Of non-productivity.
Forced to choose the enslavement
Of restricted freedom
In order to release my mind
From un-peaceful bondage.

~Oral Elixir~

I must digress into regression
To release the suppression
Of the depression
That has me repressin'
The reality that stands before me
As clear as day..
Amidst all the darkness.

My solitary confinement.
Is it really a punishment?
Or is it an assignment?
Could it be both?
The answer of the latter
Being a result of the former.
Like the prevention of being cold
Lies in the wisdom
Of knowing how to stay warmer.

While you constantly
Condemn me for past wrongs
There are plenty of bones
In the skeleton
Of your closet.

Skeletons of which I had
Not even known to have had a life

But lying in my graveyard
Tombstones have been visited by you,
And oft times put there by or for you.

So my history you know full well
But not so of yours by me.

Days

How many Days has it been,
Since the first day our eyes locked?
How many Days will it be
Til our eyes meet again?

How many Days will I spend
Thinking of you?
How many Days caught...
Drowning and sinking into you?

What shall I do?
With all those Days in between,
Now and then?
What can I do to make it seem,
That you never left...
And right here with me you've always been?

As that day draws closer,
As that day draws near.
My anxiety grows
As well as my fear.

Afraid that my eyes will overwhelm my heart
To the point of attack.
But relieved at the fact...
That the soreness of not seeing you
Is no longer a part of my sight.
Thank God for all those Days you were away
That He held on to you.
Thankful that you're alright.

Precious Time

Time, time
Precious time
Who does it belong to?
Is it yours,
Is it mine?

It's a valuable commodity
That we can either
Take,
Make,
Waste,
Or haste.

It can be too long
Or not long enough.
It can be good and smooth
Or hard and rough.

There's "quality" time,
There's "me" time.
There are times
When you want to just let go and "be" time!

There's "all work"
And "no play" time.
There's "I don't want you to leave,
Please stay" times.

There's "I'd like to get to know you better
When can we go out on a date" time.
There's "not now",
I need you to wait" times.

Time is something we can plan,
Something we can expand,
Something we can demand.
Time is something we can hold on to,
Or let slip right thru our hands.

Time can be a consequence
Of an unfortunate circumstance.
A "woulda, coulda, shoulda
If I just had another chance".

Time is promising to do better next time
Because you didn't do your best this time.

Time is
"sorry I'm late
But I'll be on time next time."
Time is "sorry but you're going to have to
Make up that time
With overtime."

Time is
"I don't have time
For that time"

There's daylight savings time
CP time
Eastern, central, mountain, pacific time.

There's last second on the clock,
Two minute warning,
Two out in the bottom ninth time.

Overtime,
Double overtime,
Extra inning
And sudden death time.

Game time
Prime time
Movie time
Hammer time

Time, time
Precious time.
Who does it belong to?

Beside Myself

Time spent with my thoughts,
Sometimes we dance
Sometimes we wrestle.
Sometimes we sit and talk.

There are times when we
Fuss and fight.
An intense battle for power!
A battle that rages
All thru the night.

There are times
When we both demand peace.
So we search for an escape,
Some time a part.
Until our energies re-peak.

There are times
When we really need to talk.
But one another
We choose to ignore.
Claiming that
What the other has said,
Has been said before.
So there's no need to say it
Or hear it anymore.

So put it on a shelf
Along with everything else
And ponder on how with me I should be dealt
Being Beside Myself.

Strange Curse

Deprived,
Denied,
But yet
Held special in God's Eyes.

Protected
But at the same time isolated.
Constantly pushing others away,
And also rejected.
Emotionally devastated.

As hours turn into days,
And days turn into years.
Aged with wisdom,
But even more so...with tears.

On an island
Surrounded by a sea of people.
Visible only in the daylight.

Mind screaming for attention.
Tongue begging to mention.
Body longing to release it's tension!

Attracting those
Not attracted too.
Not attractive
To those attracted too.

A vicious cycle
That propels itself,
Feeds itself,
Seeds itself,
But not pleasing to the self.

It's only purpose it seems...
Is to tease the self.

Not un-attractive,
But not attracting enough.
The un-attractive?
Attracting just too much.

Wanting to surrender,
But can't stand to give-up.
Finally conceding to defects,
Good fortunes comes.
In the form of false-hope appearing true.
The cycle repeats.

Now I Know

I can't re-live yesterday.
I have no guarantee on tomorrow.
All I can be sure of,
All I can grab on to,
All I can take hold of...
Is right now.
Right here,
This very moment...
This very second!
Telling you...
I love you!
Now I'm sure.
Now I Know.

Now I Know
That I loved you yesterday.
And I'm gonna love you tomorrow.
This I now know.

Everyday without you; hell!
Every hour,
Every minute,
Every second!
Has awakened the eyes of my heart.
Showing me who you are,
And what you mean to me.
Where pride and ego
Made me blind.
Now I see.

Where stubbornness and selfishness
Made me unkind.
Now I'm in need.

Now in need
Because of what I now know.
Now my mind aches
And my soul bleeds!

Now I Know

Now I know
That I can't live without you.
I may survive but,
That's not livin.
That's just existing
For the sake of being alive

Now I know that
Every breath I take
Must include you.
Every smile I make exudes
Because of you.
Every sleep from which I awake!...
I wish to be right next to you.

Call it revelation,
Call it an epiphany,
Call it profound realization!
Label it anyone of those!

Simply put...
Now I Know.

When the Time Comes

Time has taught me many things.
Time has presented itself
In many different ways.
Time has been lonely nights.
Time has been...empty days.

Time has been hours
Engaged in sexual bliss.
Time has bee a rush,
Trying to fulfill every erotic fantasy
Not wanting to miss.

Time has been mistakes.
Time has been unnecessary heartbreak.
Time has been lies.
Time has been truth...
But refusing to take.

Time has been opportunity
Knowing at the door.
Time has been too late,
The change is gone...
It's not there anymore.

Time has been lessons learned and stored.
Time has been other lessons
Not yet learned, but instead,
Completely ignored.

Time has been love gained.
Time has been love lost.
Time was unappreciated
And taken for granted.
So hard times...became the cost.

Time has been joyous.
Time has been regret.
Time has been sweet memories.
Time has been nightmares
I wish I could forget.

But in all these things...
Time has been preparation.
Another chance,
Another knock at the door.
Time presenting itself again...
Again once more.

That time is you.
But time can become us.
Time is standing before you.
So there are some things
We need to discuss.

Do you have time for me,
Better yet...we?
Is there enough time
For us to ever be?

How much of my time
Is required?
How much time,
Is enough
Before you become tired?

Can I spend my time
Making you smile?
Can I spend time with you
In your dreams?
Can we spend time in togetherness,

Walking each and every mile?
Can we stick together thru time,
No matter how long it seems?

Do you have the time for marriage?
Do you have time for the best time
Of your life?
Will you dedicate this time,
Your forever time,
By accepting this time,
And becoming "my time"?
And being my "wife"?

Now...is the Time.

The Question Remains...?

When can I see you?
When can I feel you?
When will the time come
For me to thrill you?

Where does your mind take you?
When you think of me.
Where would you like to go?
How would you like it to be?

Will I be all that you imagined?
Will the portrait fit the frame?
If not...can you adjust
To appreciate the real beauty just the same?

What will your name be?
What are some of your favorite things?
Will they be in common with mine?
Will our names have a melodic ring?

Do you even exist?
Are all my hopes and prayers in vain?
How long must I endure the pain?
The Question Remains...?

More

Of all of what you see,
There's so much more to me
So much more to be said...
So much more I can be.

More love than you can imagine
More loyalty than you would think
So much more verbal expression
Than you'll see on pad with ink.

More thought than speech
More walk than preach
More lessons to teach
More lives to reach.

More dreams than success
More hidden struggles
Than I care to attests
More pain in my heart
Than you'll ever know...
More silence, more smiles, more stress.

More blessings everyday
More opportunities coming my way
More reasons to be thankful
Even more reasons to pray.

Quilted Heart

What surrounds my heart?
Keeping it warm and safe.
The blanket of pain and disappointment
But you'd never know
Just looking at my face.

Heartache, betrayal,
Lies, deceit, and mistrust.
Just a few elements sewn together,
And the others...
Too painful to discuss.

My most tragic experience,
Are the very lessons that protect me now.
What benefit could they serve?
Let me explain how.

Pain brings about correction,
And the discipline therein
Serves as my protection.

To prevent my heart from being cold,
I took my quilt wrapped it up
Put it to bed and tucked it in.
There it'll have a chance to rest and recover
Before awakening it again.

I don't know
How long the sleep will be,
Maybe permanently.
But no one will be allowed to unwrap it...
If they're not worthy.

Undiscovered

A priceless jewel
That has been bruised,
Mishandled, and dropped
Valued at nothing...used.

All eyes are not seeing
All ears are not hearing,
Had they been in your past...
Hearts towards you would still be
endearing.

You displayed the beauty of your Heart
And shared the treasures of your Soul
Snakes and deceivers cashed in,
Then violently turned cold.

Never taking time to look
And value your true worth.
An infinite wealth of Love
That which was given to you at birth.

Between U and I

Why are there those,
Who are unknown to me,
That desire our separation
Determined not to let it be.

Our Love must be stronger,
Stronger than the hate they possess.
And if we've successful in this
All of their efforts become useless.

Will you allow them?
Will you allow them to win?
Or will you allow me
The chance to show my Love, once again.

Day by day
The wall gets higher and higher
Tricking you with delusions
Hoping to kill your desire.

I wish you had my eyes,
Because if you did, you'd cry
At the sight of what's being done
To cause division Between U and I.

An Extension of the Heart

Long awaited love
For which I prayed,
Suddenly appeared to me
My heart now slayed.

The beginning of the end?
No, the end to a new beginning.
From the moment I first saw you
All of myself you were winning.

What a happiness I felt
When you announced your intention's the same
New light shined in my heart
By the kindling of a flame.

Thoughts of your occupy my days
And dreams engulf the night.
Your eyes so beautiful and seductive
Your smile so warm and bright.

Seven days...re-named anticipation,
Satisfied merely by a sound!
Created by the wings of angels in flight.
Yes your voice is that profound.

But suddenly the rhythm changed,
Wings took flight in a different direction
Is there also a change of heart?
I can't make the connection.

Have I offended you?
Disappointed you in some way?
A mystery only you can solve,
But refuse to say.

The flame yet burns
In spite of the time apart,
So for now, there shall be silence
And yet...An Extension of the Heart.

Checking For Leaks

Inspection from the inception.
First impression is all good
At the reception.

Checking For Leaks

No rumbles, rattles, or squeaks.
This can't be true.
There has to be some fault,
Some weakness to you.

Checking For Leaks

Are you married?
Are involved?
No?
Why are you single and unattached?
This is a mystery I must solve.

Checking For Leaks

Tell me your story
So I can analyze it...
And pick it apart.
I'm gonna read between the lines.
I'm gonna discover why
No one's captured your heart.

Checking For Leaks

Since your last relationship...
Tell me...
How long has it been?
Why did it end?

Are you looking for love and commitment?
Or something casual...
Like a fuck friend.

Checking For Leaks

I'm looking, I'm listening,
I'm analyzing your every move,
Your every word.
I'll entertain every possibility
No matter how absurd.

Checking For Leaks

Dammit I can't find it!
But I know it's there!
Go ahead and tell me.
I promise I won't leave...
I swear.

Checking For Leaks

Hold up.
The answer can't be that simple.
You say you just haven't
Found the right one?
Please.
Why you lying?
That's it, I'm out of here.
I'm done!

Checking For Leaks

What?
Oh now you have something to say!
Well go ahead...I'm listening.

But I probably won't believe you anyway.

The very answer you were looking for?
The mystery you put so much energy
Into solving?
The untold story
Around which you kept revolving?
Is you!

You thought I was withholding information.
No, no, better yet,
You thought I was lying.
See, the leak wasn't in me.
It was in "your" mind.

Too busy listening for rumbles,
Rattles, and squeaks.
Instead of just enjoying the ride.
Too busy checking for leaks
That you overlook
The good things about me.
The beautiful things of me...
Standing before your very eyes.

So blinded by your own ambition
To discover my faults and weakness.
That you became arrogant in your search.
Forsaking your own humility and
meekness.

So damn sure
That I was the problem,
And determined to find it...why?
Were you looking to be
Of some help to me?
A cure.

Hell no!
You just wanted a reason
Other than yourself,
To justify your being alone.
To verify your reluctance
To see faults of your own.

You're not interested
In helping my heart.
You're more interested
In pointing out reasons
Why we should be apart.

Repair the leaks within yourself,
Instead of searching for the ones
In somebody else.

Appreciate the goodness of me,
And try to love me...
In spite of what leaks you'll find.
I'm willing to help you with yours.
If you're willing to help me with mine.

Checking For Leaks.

Missing You

It's only been a few days
Since we parted,
And the nightmares
Have already started.

Sweet memories
Attack me viciously!
The echoes of your silence
Bombard me repetitiously!

My mind in total chaos,
On the verge of madness.
And the invisibility of your beauty
Blinds me with sadness.

I'm Missing You

I miss the sound
Of my telephone ringing.
I miss the sound
Of my doorbell ringing.
I miss the sound of your voice
In the shower...singing.
I miss the wrap of the towel
To your body...clinging.

I miss picking out movies together.
I miss the debates
Of whose taste is better.

I miss our Sunday afternoon drives.
I miss us planning out our lives.

I'm still Missing You

~Oral Elixir~

I miss the way
We would tease each other with words.
The way we would please each other
By acting out those words.

I miss the long walks in the park.
I miss the naughty things we'd do
To each other after dark.

I miss the flames of satisfaction.
I miss the games of foreplay
That would create the spark.

I miss the aroma of your pleasure.
I miss diving down deep
To retrieve it's treasures.

I miss massaging your body
With hot oils and perfume.
I miss "exercising" you...
All over the room.

I miss the trembles, shakes,
And quakes
That would come...
I miss the intense love we used to make,
and the deep sleep when we were done.

I can't help it...I'm Missing You

I miss serving you
Breakfast in bed.
I miss giving you roses...dozens
All in red.

I miss your laugh.
Oh how I miss that smile.
I miss your attitude,
I miss your style.

I miss you as my queen,
I miss being your king.
I miss your hips,
Your lips...
I miss your everything!
I'm simply...Missing you.

Struck

Immediate,
And intense!
Amazed
And in complete awe!
Tried to arrange my words
To make sense.
Blown away by what I saw!

Struck!

Beautiful, yes
But there's more.
An aura,
An appeal.
Something...that makes your beauty
Even more real!
Call it what you like,
I just love the way it makes me feel!

Struck!

An attack on my nature.
I'm defenseless.
Can't escape it,
It's relentless!

Struck!

Longing to know more,
I'm asking permission to further investigate.
Hoping to be struck once again
By an inner beauty...
To help me further appreciate.

I've been "Struck"!

Across My Mustache

A gentle breeze blowing
Just for me, flowing.
To entice...no, to introduce.
Unintentional I'm sure but,
Still you seduce.

How do you expect me to react?
How should I behave?
Sweet, subtle, sensuous wave.

Your scent gives you away,
An aroma you should wear everyday.
If for no other reason
Than to make my day.

Make it last,
Make it stay,
Across my Mustache.

What's Missing

In the morning
And in the evening.
When I'm coming
And when I'm leaving
There's that void...
That emptiness that has my heart bleeding,
That has my mind disbelieving
Because my eyes have been deceiving.
Killing all hope of achieving
That which I feel
I should be receiving.
Forced to co-exist with my grieving.

The cupboards are bare
And silence permeates the air.
A conversation can't exist
Without two to share.
I can't balance myself
Because that special one...
Just isn't there.

When I need to shoulder my cry,
There's nothing but pillows there.

When I reach for comfort
In the middle of my nightmares,
There's no support for me.
No one to calm the air.

All my yesterdays
Are starting to look the same.
Monday, Tuesday, Wednesday.
All mirrors are alike,
No matter how different the frame.

What's Missing

I stand alone,
I lay alone.
I cry alone,
And I pray alone.

In the far off distance
Happiness resides under a warm sun.
And what lies in between
Is an invisible force full of resistance.
Keeping me in isolation
In spite of my persistence
To have a joyful existence.

There is a storm in my life,
A perfect storm.
It's unseen and unbeatable
It's mean and untreatable.
At least that's the way it seems.

Not Interested, But...

Not interested in a chase,
But I will pursue.
As long as you're attainable,
I'll keep after you.

Not interested in just mere sex,
But I do desire the pleasure.
There has to be more...
A spiritual connection,
To take it to the next level.

Not interested in being alone,
But I love my space.
More often than not, I'm missing you.
The tender way you kiss
Whenever we embrace.

Not interested in using you,
But at times I may need help.
Just be there in those times,
And I'll handle the next.

Familiar Ground

You'd think by now
I'd know the score.
Same thing that happened now...
Happened to me before.

Three-card Molly in effect.
Thought I picked my queen
Fooled again, wrong choice.
She vanishes from the scene.

Back on hollowed ground
Nothing but casualties to be found.
Kind spoken good-bye again the sound.
"it's not you, it's me...
Another queen will come around."
"If I could, I would. I'm just too busy now.
It's unfair to keep you tied down."

Different singer of the same song.
Heartbreaking chorus
That has played much too long.
Is there a different tune in the juke box?
Every selection it seems...
Is wrong.

What's even more sad is,
I've echoed the same question
To myself over and over again...
Why is there always a beginning,
To my heartbreaking end?

Twins Decision

Same energy
Different state.
Same flavor
Which choice do I make?

Same interest
Same flow.
Same attraction
Which way do I go?

Same desire
Same ambition.
Same attitude
Why “this” type of competition?

Same passions
Same musical taste.
Same positive effect
Neither one do I wish to waste.

How do I choose?
Who do I choose?
When will I know?
Which one to turn loose.

Solitary Heart

Enclosed in silence
Echoes of nothingness
Fills the halls.
Disturbed only
By the beat,
Bouncing off bare walls.

Hidden away in the dungeon.
Who can find it now?
Who cares enough?
Reveal yourself to me.
I dare you to be so tough!

Tucked away in the abyss,
Your tender touch I miss.
Unbalanced.
Without the weight of your heart,
Solitary confinement
Tearing my mind apart!

I hate the darkened silence
But I must adapt.
It's my environment now,
And maybe one day perhaps,
A new light will shine
And someone will really love me.
And become all mine.

But until that time
There shall be no love
Because there is no light.
So each and every day
I will struggle and fight
To hold together my heart,
For fear of it being
Permanently turn apart.

My Solitary Heart.

Why Not Me

Is not my heart allowed
To feel passion...desire?
Can I not feel attraction,
Am I not allowed
To fall victim to the weaknesses of my heart?
Even though you think it's not wise,
Because of my size.

My heart is no more immune to pain
Than yours can be.
You're in no better emotional position
Because you're smaller than me.

My fall can be just a long...
Just as hard...
And can be just as damaging
As it would be you.
In fact,
Yours might be even more so.
Because you're a bigger target.
Therefore you'll have more chances
To be disappointed...
More chances to be used and let go.

The opportunities I get
May be far fewer than yours.
But the chances I do get,
May be far truer than yours.

How dare me you say?
Nah, nah baby.
Why not me!...I say!

~Oral Elixir~

The beauty of my heart
Far out weights my size.
And the ecstasy I can provide...
Lovingly resides...
Between these big ass thighs!

Don't look at me and underestimate.
Because I can flex,
And I can stretch.
I'll have us in all type of positions.
Like a game of twister,
I'll have you damn near
Breaking your neck.

I'll have you mesmerized...
Thinking, wondering.
How could a woman her size...?

So before you jump to a wrong conclusion,
And remain ignorant in your confusion.
Take some time and recognize.
And then you'll realize.
That there is a lot more to love about me
Than just my size.

In Your Eyes

When your eyes behold me
They touch my soul in such a way
That it warms me throughout my day
And makes me want to stay
In your arms where I long to be
More often than before
Craving you more and more.

When your eyes behold me
I see passion and desire
Your temperature going higher, and higher
That spark turning to a fire
As I'm kissing you
As I only know how too
My tongue going places others can't
Your neck turned with a slight slant
As I gently bite, yet squeeze you tight
While making love to you with all my
might!

When your eyes behold me
I'm reassured
Of the value that I possess
As my fear and self-doubt are cured
Because you took the time to caress
That which needed to be.

All these things I see,
When your eyes behold me.

This

This is what I do!
This right here,
Standing right before you
Trying not to bore you.
Hoping to win over your hearts.
To simply hear you say
"I don't know you but,
As for your work, I got nothing
But mad love for you"!

This in no way
Is done for "vain" purposes,
So please don't misunderstand.
This is done for "pain" purposes!
This is done to help "sustain" purposes!

I have to answer that voice,
That calls, that burning from deep within!
It's mandatory,
That I submit to that yearning
To write and to speak...
Over and over again.

This is a sickness for me
It's like a woman
Who's blessed with thickness to me.

It's beautiful!
It's sexy!
It's seductive!

Got me like a crack head
Fiending for a hit!
Because the more I write,

~Oral Elixir~

The more I become
Addicted to this shit!

This is what defines me!
This is what refines me!
This is where you can find me!

I'll say it again!
In case you weren't listening.

This is what defines me!
This is what refines me!
This is where you can find me!

I eat this,
I drink this,
I sleep this,
And dream this!

I'm like hundred children
In one room at a birthday party
After having cake and ice creaming this!

And for those of us
Who've been in room with only five or six
It's enough to make you pick-up
A belt, a bat, a few bricks!

So just imagine a hundred
Of them little jokers
Running thru your head!
Constantly, all day long
From morning
Til it's time to go to bed!

But it doesn't stop there!
It awakes me out of my sleep!
Saying "I got something to say,
Write this down, man this is deep!"

See ya'll think I'm kidding.
How do you think I came up with this
piece?!
Hell, this one snatched me right
Out of my sleep!

Me without this
Is like a crime to me!
And it's punishable by death!
So you see...
This is a must have.
This is a must be.
This is Poetry!
And Poetry...is Me!

Time

More precious than diamonds,
Platinum and gold.
The pleasure of growing old.
Time.
Something we have very little of,
Something we take no advantage of.
Time.

Time with our children,
Is there ever enough?
Idle time...
There's much too much.

How much time do we need?
How much do we deserve?

To Be Found

Forever finding
But never binding.
Elusive and evasive.
Constantly on the look out,
Always listening but...
No one's been too persuasive.

I'm in a place
Not to be seen,
But, I'm not at all missing.
I'm constantly standing here before you
And yet it seems...

Absent Without Leaving

We're sleeping in the same bed,
But nothing's being said.
We're breathing the same air,
But the life in it is dead.

We dine at the same table,
But yet in still we're not able,
To consume adequate amounts
Of conversation.

I can't seem to touch you anymore
Without first making a reservation.

Love

Love is a verb.
Meaning…it's a thing of action,
A thing that causes movement.
It's a motivator,
It gives rise to improvement.

It's a two edged sword
That can cut both ways.
It can create the loneliest nights,
And the brightest days.

Love can impress,
Suppress.
Cause you to digress, and regress.
Make you undress.
Give you reason to better dress.
Give rise to suspiciousness
Making you a better detective
Than Elliot Ness.

"Beyond Sex"

I'm gonna get straight to the point...
I want U!
I'm not trying to rush the sex,
because sex should never be rushed.
It should be taken in slowly,
with a sense of enjoyment.
Not empty & unfulfilled
like unemployment.
Because I'm ready to put in some work.
I'm talking about over a period of time,
which includes overtime.
And where I wanna take U...
is gonna take some time.
Would U like to know where I wanna take U?

Beyond Sex

I wanna take U into the unknown.
Into "deep" undiscovered erogenous zones.

I wanna go beyond those familiar sensations,
and create new temptations.
Because deep within U
there are new pleasures to find.
Pleasures that go beyond the physical...
I'm talking about your mind.
Because anybody can bump & grind,
but not everyone can pleasure your mind.

Causing U to have multiple mental orgasms.
Sexual mind spasms...
which not only makes your pussy wet,
but also causes your brain to sweat.

Beyond Sex

I wanna take U deep into space.
I'm talking about a place
well into the universe.
A place GOD has yet to create.
A place when creation is made...
U & I would see it first.

Beyond Sex

I wanna take U to your most extreme fantasy.
I want us to re-define ecstasy,
I want us to re-design sensuality,
I want us to re-fine sexuality.

Beyond Sex

I wanna take U Beyond Sex
to where just the thought of me
causes U to lose your breath.
Hearing my voice
makes U cum all over yourself.
Just seeing me...
makes your clitoris erect!

I want it to be to where,
if someone were to ask U to give a description,
All U can do is show them your prescription.
Because it's an addiction

that only I can fix!
An addiction satisfied only with my dick!

A lick!
A lick so satisfying...
that I've tattooed my tongue across your clit!

Beyond Sex

I want U to experience total ecstasy
from head to toe.
I want it to be so
that when U cum,
U can't seem to stop.
And when U do...
U beg to cum some mo'.

Beyond Sex.

"All I Want Is The Fantasy"

I know this may sound bold but,
I want something from U...
but it's not what U think.
Yes I want to get close to U...
get next to U...
get beside U...
but I'm not talking about sexin' U.

Let me explain what it is U do to me.
Your beauty "alone" makes my heart dance.
Your voice makes my ears erect,
vibrates my soul,
and awakens the hairs on the back of neck.
The perfume U wear...
arouses me in such a way
til I can't breathe without U being there.

You've given me the most beautiful feeling
of sensuous arousal,
eroticism ,
and sexual excitement...
and you've never even touched me!
You're a fantasy!
But you're a fantasy I can see,
Hear, feel, and touch.

I've "been" with some women
that haven't aroused me half as much!

But I'm not asking U
to be with me in that way.

All I Want Is The Fantasy
I want my heart to continue dancing
to this new rhythm that you've set.
I want U to continue sending out those vibrations
that roll thru my very soul.
Just talk to me,
say what U say in that way that U do.
Whether it be an encyclopedia of words,
or merely a word or two.

All I Want Is The Fantasy

I want U to touch me,
nothing extreme,
nothing intimate...
a simple hug will do.
Holding my hand will do.
Anything beyond that...
my imagination can do.
Because in my imagination...
our intimacy is perfect,
our lovemaking is perfect.
There is no disappointing me...
There is no disappointing U.

Every kiss is perfection.
Every stroke is perfection.
Every orgasm is perfection.
Each and every time...
is perfection.

All I Want Is The Fantasy

I want to inhale U.
I want to take U in deep.
Take U into my lungs
so U can be the oxygen that sustains me,
the oxygen that breathes life into me.
I want your perfume to color the portraits
that paint my fantasies of U.

All I Want Is The Fantasy

I just want to look at U,
behold U,
And allow your beauty
to do all the wonderful things it can do.
Like remind me of how awesome GOD is.
To see and to behold
that which originated in GOD'S imagination.
Your beauty helps me to appreciate the beauty of GOD.

All I Want Is The Fantasy

I only need some of your time,
I don't need it all.
I only need enough.
Enough to keep my heart dancing.
Enough to sustain my imagination.
Enough to behold your beauty.
Enough to maintain the Fantasy.

All I Want Is The Fantasy

"I've Had Women"

I've had a lot things in my life.
Money,
cars,
fancy apartments,
good jobs...
hell I even had a wife.

I've had clothes,
shoes,
parties,
and backyard barbeques!

But...
of all the things I've had...
I've Had Women!
That's right...
I've Had Women!

I've had tall women,
short women,
fat women,
skinny women,
ugly women,
and pretty women.

I've had thick women,
thin women,
Dark,
Cocoa-brown,
Carmel,
and Light-skinned women.

I've Had Women
with tight asses,
phat asses,
round asses,
and flat asses.

Women with wide hips,
women with slim hips.
Women with thick lips,
women with thin lips,
and women with just the right lips.

I'll say it again...
I've Had Women.
But I'm not thru!

I've had freaky women,
sexy women,
nympho women,
and women who like women too!

I've beautiful women,
cute women,
runway model women,
I mean drop-dead gorgeous women!

I've Had Women
with long hair,
short hair,
straight hair,
nappy hair,
fake hair,
and women with "that" much hair.

I've Had Women
with big breast,
Women with small breast.
Women with huge breast,
and women with almost not at all breast.

I've had corporate women,
blue collar women.
Police women,
nurse women,
stripper women,
teacher women,
and preacher women.

I've had slutty women,
saved women,
nutty women,
and depraved ass women.

Ain't nothing like women!

I've had good women,
bad women,
happy women,
And sad women.
Mean women,
glad women,
quiet women,
loud women,
and down right mad ass women.

I've Had Women
who were loyal to me.
Women that were "there" for me.
Women that toiled for me,
women that spoiled me,

and women that never cared for me.

I've Had Women
that used me,
women that abused me.
women that schooled me,
and women that made a damn fool of me!

I've had boo-gee women,
diva women,
ghetto women,
sista-girl finger snappin',
hand on the hip,
neck twirlin' round-the-way women.
Even the over-religious
"I'm saving it for my wedding day" women.

Now don't be confused...
these are just a large combination
that add up to only a few.

In all my "having",
I never fully grasped
what it truly meant "to have".

Now all that I do have
are those descriptions of what I did have...
of what I could haved,
if only I would haved,
now knowing that I should haved.
Now my heart,
my vision,
and my ambitions have all changed.
My priorities...
have been re-arranged.

Now...
I have but 1 ambition,
1 desire.
To become 1,
with that special 1,
and stay 1...
til death do us come.

"Picture This"

Visualize...
Fantasize...
Listen...
Because I want U to conceptualize
the many things I see
when U stand in the light of my eyes.

Teasing me,
pleasing me.
Mental images of U & I intertwined...
seizing me.

Imagination arrested...
freezing me.
In a place I long to be physically.
Desperately longing to make that place my reality.

Picture This

Lips moist & wet,
breast full & erect.
Between your thighs U sweat.
Images only in my mind and yet...
all three provide a real place
for me to lay my face...
to sample and to taste.

Just let me taste it,
I promise I won't waste it.

Let me kiss U there,
down there where it counts.
I swear I'll drink every ounce!

Can U Picture This?

I don't want U to just feel
my velvet tongue sliding across your clit.
or the full blooded stiffness of my dick
separating your clit.

I also want U to feel,
I mean really feel,
the level of energy I'm producing
to keep your energy level high.
To make sure orgasms are constantly reproducing.

You're more than a Picture.
You're a masterpiece
with no need for a frame.
Because your sensuality and your erotica has no borders.
And therefore can't be contained.

You're more than erotic,
more than sensual,
more than sexual.
You're an education
mastered in all three,
with a degree...
for satisfying me.

"Something I Miss"

Charged in an instant
by the most powerful kiss!
Laid out,
stretched out,
nipples hard & erect!
An inner voice from the past asking...
What is this?
I'm searching for an answer.
But for now...
I'll continue to lay back
and wait for what's next.

As my pussy throbs
With juices flowing,
long overdue orgasms cum near.
The answer to the question is clear...
This is something I want!
This is something I need!
This is something I miss!
This "something" all started...
The first time my lips
touched his lips.

So what am I to do now?
Passion like this hasn't cum
since I don't know when.
But here it is...
reminding me of how.

Now only how,
But why?

~Oral Elixir~

How did I get along without it?
Why did I go so long in silence?
Denying my body he pleasure
of shouting about it!

Now I and these questions
Have come face to face.
But now it's another man's face
standing in my man's place.
Causing me to have a quagmire...
Do I stick & stay and play dead?
Or do I resuscitate and replace?

How can I return to the grave
knowing that passion does exist?
How can I deny myself knowing that...
This is Something I Miss.

Why should I return to a dead state
when my man no longer
has the desire to
facilitate,
operate,
or demonstrate!

How can I live
without that which reminds me
that I'm alive?

Why shouldn't I live,
instead of just survive?
Should I continue with what's missing?
Or simply...
miss out?

Pressure Points

Allow me to be candid
About a very important matter.
To some...it may embarrass,
And some others...maybe even flatter.

There are some
Who'll be surprised.
A few will find it appealing.
Some will come alive.
And to the rest...
Most revealing!

I'm talking about Pressure Points.

Those places that release
Passions deep within.
Like warm honey on the tongue
Gliding across smooth skin.

Earlobes and toes,
Belly-buttons and tongue probes...
From the small of the back,
All the way up the spine.
Tender bites on the lip,
Firm bites on the behind.

Pressure Points

The breast and inner thigh,
Velvet tongue on the clit
So good makes you wanna cry!
Is that your spot?
Yeah, that's it!

Pressure Points

Just name it...
I'll tame it
Then claim it,
Nail it to the wall
Frame it and re-name it!

Pressure Points

While I'm smacking it from the rear,
Orgasms come near,
Toes tighten and curl,
Pillow talking in your ear
Voices peaking
Bed squeaking
So loud til the neighbors hear!

Pressure Points discovered
Pressure Points found
Pressure Point your lover,
Unlimited pressures...abound.

About the Author Ausar, Lord of the Perfect Black

The world's awakening is not by a hot cup of coffee, but by the sensual, soul stirring, nerve vibrating, mind blowing and breath taking poems of Ausar. A floetic poet with a great stage presence introduced himself to poetry to help cope with a break-up. The first young woman he ever gave his heart to, broke his heart by leaving him for another man with more with money. With pen in hand, Ausar took his feelings to the paper. In an instant, his poetic flow filled the pages to the entire notebooks end. It was there that Ausar had a newfound love...POETRY!

On the spoken word tip, it was back in 1998 when Ausar saw a spoken word performance. The *"word bug"* bit him so deeply that it left a very powerful, spirit-filling serum that would allow this *'Lord of the Perfect Black'* to spit out poems that would influence the world. Ausar's poetry includes topics that range from love, romance, erotica, social consciousness, religion and spirituality, black consciousness, and family issues.

Ausar first entered the world of spoken word in 1998 in the city of St. Louis where a bite by the "spoken word bug" occurred. His performances include Legacy, The Haraambe Institute, Raw Sugar, The Afrikan Village, and Lyrics of the Lou, all in the city of St. Louis where many received him with open arms! Ausar moved to the city of Atlanta in the year 2000 where he got heavily involved on the spoken word set. He performed at various venues around the Atlanta Metro area for a couple of years before producing & hosting his own spoken word show at the C'est Bon Cajun Restaurant Bar & Grill in Lithonia, GA. Some of Atlanta's top spoken word artist came to perform at his show. Those who came thru to spit include Def Poetry artist Abyss, Dana Gilmore, Jon Goode, and Tommy Bottoms. Last but not least, Cocktails, Freedom Speaks, and Khari B. (Chicago).

The spoken word CD for ***Oral Elixir*** will soon follow. The CD will only add true definition to this talented, creative, mind stimulating work. So keep your ears prepared for the delightful, soul-stirring, erotic sounds of Oral Elixir. For these spoken words delivered by Ausar's heavy, deep, but smooth voice and driven passion will send you to a land of liberation and sexual exploitation. Be it all by yourself...or someone else, the CD will take you there.

To contact Ausar about performances, and book signings/spoken word parties, you can e-mail him at ImAusar@go.com, www.myspace.com/talk2ausar or visit his website: www/theperfectblack.com

Aminia Books
and
Publishing
If you believe...WE believe!

Aminia Books
and
Publishing
If you believe...WE believe!

Notes

Notes

Notes

Printed in the United States
201026BV00005B/13-24/A

9 780979 915499